THE CENTRAL SCHOOL OF SPEECH AND DRAMA

UNIVERSITY OF LONDON

Please return or renew this item by the last date shown.

The Library, Central School of Speech and Drama,
Embassy Theatre, Eton Avenue, London, NW3 3HY
http://heritage.cssd.ac.uk
library@cssd.ac.uk
Direct line: 0207 559 3942

WILLIAM MACTAGGART 1903–1981

SPONSORED BY

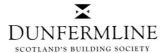

DUNFERMLINE

SCOTLAND'S BUILDING SOCIETY

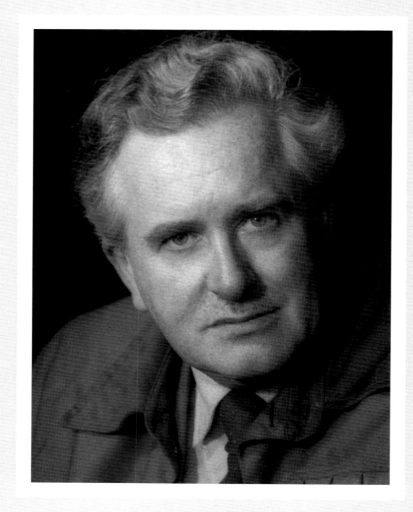

William MacTaggart *circa* 1962

WILLIAM MacTAGGART

1903–1981

BY IAIN GALE

NATIONAL GALLERIES OF SCOTLAND
1998

Published by the Trustees
of the National Galleries of Scotland
for the exhibition *William MacTaggart 1903–1981*
held at the Scottish National Gallery of Modern Art
Edinburgh, 14 February – 10 May 1998

Designed and typeset in Monotype Plantin by Dalrymple
Printed by BAS Printers, Over Wallop

Front cover:
Detail from *Danish Harbour, circa* 1960
[catalogue 28]

Back cover:
MacTaggart at work in his Drummond Place studio
circa 1957

Dunfermline Building Society
is an award winner under the Pairing Scheme
(the National Heritage Arts Sponsorship Scheme)
for its support of this exhibition.

The Pairing Scheme is a Government Scheme
managed by ABSA (Association for Business
Sponsorship of the Arts).

Preface

Thirty years ago, in 1968, the Scottish Arts Council and National Galleries of Scotland combined to mount an important retrospective of over sixty works by William MacTaggart. The exhibition opened at the Scottish National Gallery of Modern Art, in those days located at Inverleith House, and was the first in that venue to be devoted to a living Scottish artist.

By that time MacTaggart was recognised internationally not only as a gifted painter but also as a vital figure in the promotion of the arts in his native country. Early in his career he had been instrumental in organising an exhibition of the work of Edvard Munch for the Society of Scottish Artists. In his positions as President of that Society and of the Royal Scottish Academy, and through his involvement in the early history of the Arts Council of Great Britain and Edinburgh International Festival, he was directly involved in bringing to Scotland an outstanding series of exhibitions of work by artists such as Klee, Vuillard and Bonnard, Cézanne, Renoir, Braque and Gauguin, as well as promoting the art of his fellow Scots.

The present exhibition is the first to be dedicated to William MacTaggart's own work in a public museum since the 1968 show. We are greatly indebted to those who, in the past, have presented or bequeathed pictures to our own collections, all of which are included here; and to the museums, galleries, corporate collections and the many private owners who have so generously lent to this exhibition.

William MacTaggart is the fourth in our series on the major figures of the Edinburgh School, following William Gillies (1994), William Crozier (1995), and Anne Redpath (1996). It has been selected by Iain Gale who has also written the introductory essay in the accompanying catalogue; we are very grateful for his contribution. Among National Galleries staff who have assisted in various ways, we would like to single out Philip Long who has been responsible for the organisation of the exhibition and Janis Adams who has produced the catalogue. Our thanks also for their help are due to: Tom Bell, Tom Bell Fine Art, Troon; Graham Harris, The Blythswood Gallery, Glasgow; Patrick Bourne, Bourne Fine Art, Edinburgh; Bernard Williams and Neil MacRae, Christie's Scotland Limited; Selina Skipwith, Robert Fleming Holdings Limited; Alison Geissler; Ann Macandrew; Harriet Macandrew; Sheila MacTaggart; Tilly Marshall; Ewan Mundy, Ewan Mundy Fine Art, Glasgow; Iain Gordon Brown, National Library of Scotland; Joanna Soden, Royal Scottish Academy; Guy Peploe and Iain Barnett, The Scottish Gallery, Edinburgh; Véronique Gunner, Sotheby's, London; and Duncan Macmillan, University of Edinburgh.

Finally, we would like to thank Dunfermline Building Society. Our association with the Society began in 1995 when they generously agreed to sponsor our William Crozier exhibition. This was followed by their sponsorship in 1996-7 of Anne Redpath and we were delighted when they agreed to return this year a third time to support the current exhibition of William MacTaggart.

TIMOTHY CLIFFORD
Director, National Galleries
of Scotland

RICHARD CALVOCORESSI
Keeper, Scottish National Gallery
of Modern Art

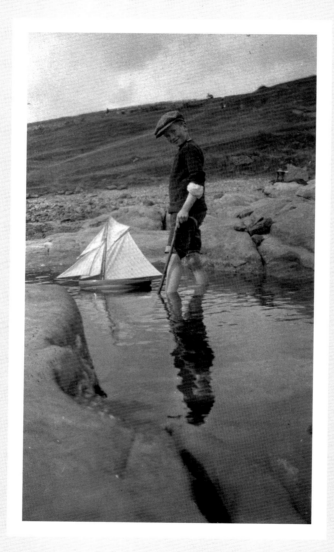

figure 1 William MacTaggart *circa* 1914

Introduction

IT was, on the whole, a positive review, particularly for the work of so young an artist. 'Some of the pictures', it enthused, 'show skilful use of colour'. There was, it continued, 'a general impression of vigour and sincerity and robust individuality...'.[1] Praise indeed from the conservatively-minded *The Scotsman* newspaper. Presciently too, the anonymous critic of this first solo exhibition had hit upon the salient features of the work of William MacTaggart, which would mark him out, over the coming fifty years, as one of Scotland's greatest twentieth-century artists.

William MacTaggart [figure 1] was born on 15 May 1903 at Loanhead in Midlothian, the elder son of Hugh MacTaggart and Roberta Little. He was named after his uncle William, who had died, tragically young, at sea. William's father, Hugh, was a marine engineer – co-founder of MacTaggart and Scott – who later specialised in submarine construction for the war effort. The boy grew up with his two older sisters, Mary and Margaret, and younger brother Hugh in a happy family home, with an adoring mother and a father he was later to describe as 'a very splendid chap and generous'.[2] This generosity, though, was tempered with a late-Victorian sense of propriety which kept him from any real intimacy with his son. Yet, for all its comfort and order, this would not have been a necessarily promising environment for a nascent painter, had it not been for a singular advantage: MacTaggart's paternal grandfather was none other than his namesake, William McTaggart (1835–1910)[figure 2], the distinguished Scottish landscape painter.[3] Hillwood, the family house, was filled with his work. Hugh and Berta had been given a large seascape by Hugh's father as a wedding present and thereafter, whenever finances permitted, they would purchase other works – generally from Alexander Reid in Glasgow. So extensive did their collection become, that by 1914 Hugh had constructed what he referred to, with characteristic reticence, as the 'billiard room', but which was in fact a gallery, principally for his father's work. Its presence was a huge formative influence on young William, who recalled in a later interview that he had once remarked to 'the old boy' (his grandfather, who died when he was aged seven), that he was 'going to be a painter like my grandfather'.[4]

Alongside the McTaggarts, Hugh also hung works by Boudin and minor French Impressionists and it was this school, with its concern with the depiction of light and fleeting sensation, which provided William's first taste of what art was about. It is significant that some three years after the gallery was built, Hugh should have constructed in the garden what he, again with some dissemblance, referred to as a 'summer house' – a euphemism for a studio for his son, who, at the age of fourteen, was already showing considerable artistic promise. To the boy's further advantage was the fact that his father, through his own comfortable upbringing, was aware that painting could be a worthwhile profession.[5] It also must have seemed to his parents a suitable occupation for a boy who was, from the age of four, following a serious bronchial illness, plagued by chronic ill health.[6]

MacTaggart's earliest traceable work is a painting of a ploughed field at Woodhouselee, west of Loanhead, done in 1919, at the age of sixteen [plate 1]. An interesting, planar composition, it seems to owe little to McTaggart senior, but looks instead to French artists of the 1880s. It also recalls, in its measured brushwork, its colour range and the way in which the foreground appears to approach the viewer, the paintings of Vincent van Gogh (1853–90), produced at Arles in the summer of 1888 [figure 3].[7] Although MacTaggart later firmly denied, with specific reference to *The Ploughed Field, Woodhouselee*,

having seen the work of Van Gogh at this date, such is the similarity that an indirect, even subconscious influence cannot be ruled out.[8] Perhaps he had learnt of Van Gogh's work through his father's acquaintance with the dealer Alexander Reid, who had known the artist personally and had dealt in his work since the 1890s.[9] What is almost certain is that at this early date MacTaggart was quite unaware of the work of the German Expressionists (whose painting in fact he always regarded as 'frightfully brutal').[10] The fact that this painting should also appear to have something in common with the early landscapes of Max Pechstein (1881–1955) [figure 4], suggests rather a common urge to expression (remarkable in such a young man) and a mutual debt to Van Gogh.

The Ploughed Field, according to the present owner (the son

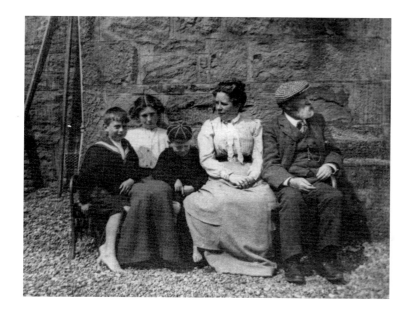

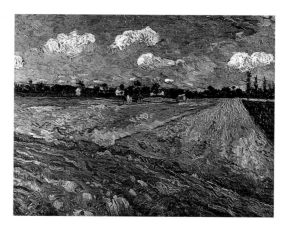

figure 2 The MacTaggart Family *left to right:* Ivor, Maisie, William, Roberta and William senior, *circa* 1907

figure 3 Vincent van Gogh *Ploughed Fields*, 1888 oil on canvas, 72.5 × 92cm Vincent van Gogh Museum, Amsterdam

of the original purchaser who was a family friend of the MacTaggarts), was regarded by William as the first painting he considered worth selling. It is significant that it should have been painted the year MacTaggart entered Edinburgh College of Art. After a lonely childhood spent in private tutelage at home, he now found himself in good company. William Gillies (1898–1973), having been diverted by war service, had just returned to student life and, despite being some five years MacTaggart's senior, now became a close friend, along with fellow students William Geissler (1896–1963) and William Crozier (1893–1930). Their mutual influence is of paramount importance in understanding MacTaggart's early development.

Although to describe young William [figure 5] as a rebel

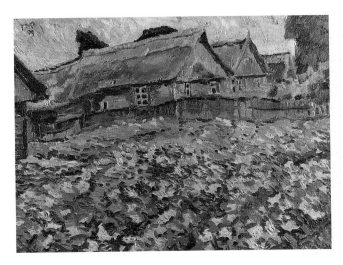

figure 4 Max Pechstein *Morning*, 1909
oil on canvas, 50.5 × 65.3cm
private collection

might be a misnomer, *The Ploughed Field* was hardly typical of the artistic style being taught at Edinburgh in the early years of the twentieth century. Head of the School of Drawing and Painting at the time was David Alison (1882–1955), who was concerned primarily with gradation of tone. Draughtsmanship was all-important and was taught well by the likes of David Foggie (1878–1948) – disciple of Degas and Ingres – who, according to MacTaggart, 'spent most of his time trying to prove that Cézanne could not draw'.[11] Perhaps more in keeping with MacTaggart's youthful enthusiasm was the composition master, John Duncan (1866–1945), whose interest in French Symbolism might even be seen as an early influence. Given this aesthetic climate, it is arguable that MacTaggart's ill health might have been his passport to artistic originality. For, had this not restricted him to attending only on a part-time basis, despite an undeniable strength of character, he might have missed the chance to experiment at this crucial stage, a quality which is so evident in *The Ploughed Field*.

MacTaggart remained at the College of Art until 1921. In that year he exhibited his first work at the Royal Scottish Academy – a landscape entitled *Early Spring*. Within two years he had been elected a member of the Society of Scottish Artists and set himself up in a studio at 45 Frederick Street along with William Crozier, a haemophiliac, with whom he probably sensed a camaraderie born of ill health. Their room looked out across the ordered rooftops of Edinburgh's New Town. The view was a perfect foil for Crozier's Cubism [figure 6] and it is hardly surprising that MacTaggart's work of the 1920s has been said to demonstrate the influence of the older artist.[12]

In 1923, together with Crozier, Gillies and Geissler and seven others, MacTaggart founded the 1922 Group, so named from the year in which most of them had received their Diplomas. For the next eight years the group exhibited annually at the New Gallery in Edinburgh's Shandwick Place. Of their first

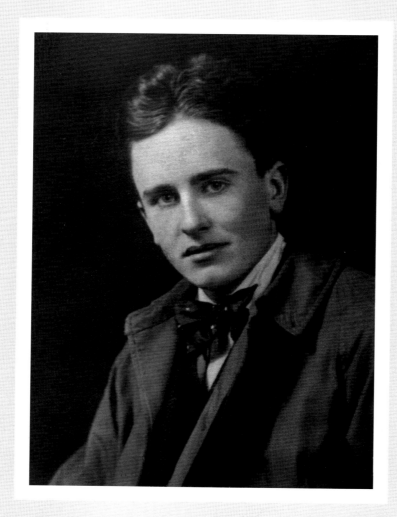

figure 5 William MacTaggart *circa* 1920

showing, *The Scotsman* commented that their colour seemed 'finer and fuller in quality than what we have seen in the pictures of their immediate elders.'[13] It seems a curious comment if one considers the coolly analytical nature of Crozier's work, which was about to receive even greater encouragement.

In December 1923 Crozier, leaving MacTaggart behind, travelled to Paris where he joined Gillies and Geissler (already there on scholarships) in the studio of André Lhote – the Académie Montparnasse. A Cubist, less radical than Picasso and Gris, Lhote [figure 7] had created a form of realism tempered by Cubist principles of formal analysis which held a strong attraction for a generation of Scottish painters. MacTaggart later admitted that he had wanted to go with the others to study under Lhote but was unable to do so due to a recurrence of his chest problems.[14] According to Gillies, however, he did not miss much and, in the long term, this lost op-

portunity may have proved a blessing.[15] MacTaggart would learn of Cubism from Crozier and that distancing would eventually make it all the easier to cast off such formalist constraints.

MacTaggart visited France in 1922. He went to Cannes with his mother just before New Year and stayed about six weeks. It is from this time that we can date *La Croisette, Cannes* [figure 8], his painting of the promenade. MacTaggart worked on the spot, travelling to his chosen locations by bus or train, with a little satchel of paints and a small easel. While *La Croisette*, only ten by fourteen inches in size, follows the fluid, loose style of *The Ploughed Field*, another work of the same trip, *Cork Oaks, Le Cannet* [figure 9], is more obviously Post-Impressionist, almost Fauve in feeling. As he neared the end of his stay MacTaggart decided to show the thirty odd works he had painted and to this end he hired the hall of St Andrew's, the

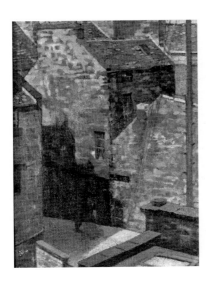 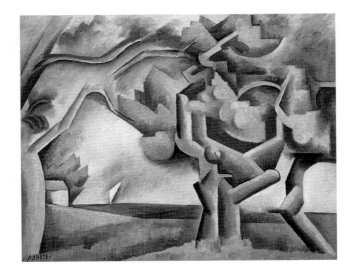

figure 6 *left*
William Crozier
Thistle Street Mews,
1923, oil on canvas,
61.2 × 45.7cm
Perth Museum and
Art Gallery

figure 7 *right*
André Lhote
*Paysage du Bassin
d'Arcachon, circa* 1915
oil on canvas,
59.6 × 73.6cm
private collection

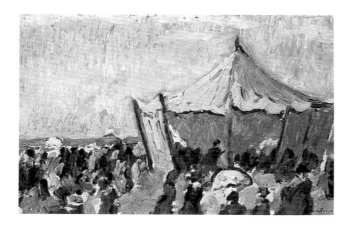

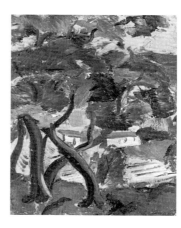

figure 8 *left*
William MacTaggart
La Croisette, Cannes,
1923, oil on canvas,
25.4 × 35.6cm
private collection

figure 9 *right*
William MacTaggart
Cork Oaks, Le Cannet,
1923, oil on canvas,
35.6 × 30.5cm
private collection

Scottish church in Cannes. It was 'a rather amateurish affair … though the paintings had nothing amateurish about them'.[16] After the show had closed William and his mother went to Italy for six weeks, from early February to mid March 1923, and it was here that he probably painted the work shown at the Royal Scottish Academy in 1924, entitled simply *Florence*.[17] It seems, on the strength of this, that it might have been on Mac-Taggart's advice that, in 1924, Crozier, Gillies and Geissler, then still in France, also travelled to Florence.

The winter of 1923–4 was again spent in Cannes with his mother.[18] Back in Edinburgh, however, with the return of his three friends from Paris in October 1924, things began to change. Crozier, who had come back laden with monographs on such innovators as Derain, Vlaminck and Friesz, now began to fill MacTaggart's head with as yet unimagined imagery and principally with Lhote's philosophy. This was essentially formulaic and concerned with balance. It was a way of seeing in which every curve must be complemented by a straight line. MacTaggart quickly assimilated the ideas, and

they continued to inform his painting over the next six years.

Throughout the 1920s and 1930s MacTaggart divided his time between Scotland and France, where he spent two to three months every winter. His first unaccompanied trip was in late 1924 to Cassis and, perhaps in the face of this new freedom, the paintings he made were very different – more stagey, more tightly composed, building on Crozier's ideas, and with heavier outlines reminiscent of Cézanne, the Fauves and Matisse. These paintings might also reflect a new awareness of Roger Fry's Post-Impressionist essays in *Vision and Design*, first published in 1919 and of Clive Bell's still influential *Significant Form in Art*, which had been widely available since 1914.

From 1925 to 1929, the companion on MacTaggart's French trips was Crozier and a number of important early works date from this period in which MacTaggart can be seen to be consolidating his early style. Here again, in intimate records of Grimaud [plate 2], the picturesque little town in the hills above St Tropez, and Bormes-les-Mimosas, the influence of Crozier, Cézanne and Lhote is evident. The two artists also visited Anne Redpath (1895–1965) and her husband James Michie, the architect. Redpath, eight years MacTaggart's senior, had graduated from Edinburgh College of Art in 1918 and had, since around 1928, been living in some splendour at St-Raphaël.[19]

The paintings of Crozier and MacTaggart at this time make an interesting comparison, sharing a similarly pale tonal range and a simplification of form reminiscent of Roger Fry and the English Bloomsbury artists. MacTaggart's *Bormes-les-Mimosas* shows a similar fascination with planar abstraction to that expressed by Crozier in his Edinburgh studio painting [see figure 6]. The palette though, is Cézanne's, of around 1880. But also, importantly, there is evidence of a knowledge of André Dunoyer de Segonzac (1884–1974), that elusive French landscape and still-life painter whose freedom of handling and colour had recently influenced Vanessa Bell (1879–1961) and Duncan Grant (1885–1978).

Segonzac, whose own style can be traced to Cézanne and the Fauves, was little-known in Scotland, but was familiar to French audiences and had showed at the Independent Gallery

in London in 1923. He favoured an earthy palette and a somewhat staccato effect achieved by the use of a palette knife and heavy impasto. It has also been suggested that S.J. Peploe (1871–1935) may have influenced Crozier's approach to landscape at this time.[20] Crozier reviewed a show of Peploe's work at Aitken Dott in Edinburgh in December 1927 and expressed admiration for his limited tonal range.[21] Both Peploe and Segonzac certainly affected the appearance of MacTaggart's works of this period, in such paintings as *Grimaud* [plate 2] and *The Gate in the Wood* [plate 4]. It is possible to see in *La Croisette* and other works of the earlier 1920s an affinity with Peploe's Royan paintings of 1910 [figure 10] and those he made at Etaples in 1907. Indeed, all three artists were painting in the Cassis area in the mid 1920s and MacTaggart later admitted having visited Peploe while in Antibes to spend a day with him. It seems improbable that the older artist did not have some influence on, or at least an interest for, the two young men – although, as MacTaggart was fond of saying, 'we are all the children of Cézanne'.[22]

In 1928, however, a curious change took place in the work

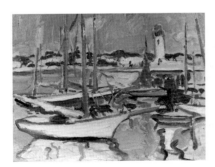

figure 10 S.J. Peploe *Boats at Royan*, 1910 oil on board, 27 × 34.9cm Scottish National Gallery of Modern Art

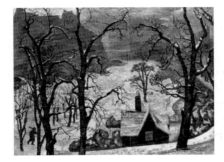

figure 11 William Crozier *Edinburgh in Snow*, *circa* 1928, oil on canvas, 71.3 × 91.5cm Scottish National Gallery of Modern Art

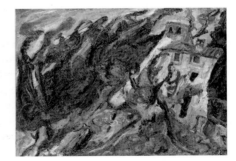

figure 12 Chaïm Soutine *Les Gorges du Loup*, *circa* 1921–3, oil on canvas, 62.8 × 86.3cm Scottish National Gallery of Modern Art

of both MacTaggart and Crozier. From the coolness of *Edinburgh (from Salisbury Crags)*, his masterpiece of around 1927, Crozier now moved to *Edinburgh in Snow* [figure 11], with its Bruegelesque feel and increased use of impasto. MacTaggart at the same time made a move towards a looseness of handling in *Snow, near Lasswade* [plate 6]. It was as if analysis was threatened by an instinctive yearning for expression. And perhaps this suggests that both men were looking elsewhere – possibly to recent developments in France, for example in the expressive landscapes of Chaïm Soutine (1893–1943) [figure 12],[23] and more specifically to a northern Romantic tradition of landscape painting.[24]

It is also significant that in 1927 MacTaggart was elected to the Society of Eight which at that time included Sir John Lavery (1856–1941), Peploe and F.C.B. Cadell (1883–1937). It is not unreasonable to surmise that Peploe, so recently encountered in the south of France, might have been instrumental in his election.

As 1929 dawned, Crozier and MacTaggart again prepared to travel together abroad. For MacTaggart it was to be a successful year. His first solo show at Aitken Dott was well received. There were twenty-eight works, varying from four to twenty-five guineas in price and ranging from still lifes to views of Machrihanish and other Scottish subjects, including *Snow, near Lasswade*. In his catalogue introduction, MacTaggart's exact contemporary and erstwhile fellow pupil at Edinburgh College of Art, Henry Harvey Wood, noted that 'MacTaggart Yr' (the Younger, as he then signed himself) was 'a painter of vigour, sensibility and real originality, in his natural and spontaneous reaction to the world around him … If sincerity, directness of statement, refinement of design and colour, and vigour of form are qualities that have any value in painting … the work of William MacTaggart deserves your attention.'[25]

In bitter contrast to the elation brought by this praise, MacTaggart faced the tragedy of personal loss. The following year, 1930, his father was taken ill and died. Within three months his mother too was dead. The third catastrophe came in December with the all-too-predictable death, as a result of his haemophilia, of William Crozier.

Although Gillies subsequently moved into the Frederick Street studio which, some accounts have it, the two artists now shared, MacTaggart later recalled having left it to move back to the family home at Loanhead. Whatever the situation, Gillies was not as close to MacTaggart as Crozier had been. It does not seem fanciful to conclude that it might have been the mood of tragic introspection pervading MacTaggart's life at this time which made him turn even more decisively to the work of another artist, Edvard Munch, exhibited at the Society of Scottish Artists (SSA) in the winter of 1931–2.

Throughout this time of bereavement, MacTaggart's spirits were lifted by a new friendship, which had begun in France, some time between 1924 and 1928. Miss Fanny Margaretha Basilier Aavatsmark was a young and attractive Norwegian. An aspiring art critic, she had been sent out to the south of France to act as society hostess for her uncle, the Norwegian Consul. The daughter of General Ivar Aavatsmark[26] and a Swedish singer, she was cultured, intelligent and lively. MacTaggart was immediately taken with her. Curiously though, it was not to William that she became attached but to his friend and fellow artist, Harold Morton, to whom she was soon engaged. In 1929, 1930 and 1931 Morton visited Fanny in Oslo, and it is possible that MacTaggart accompanied him.[27] For, apart from their friendship with Fanny, the two artists were drawn to Scandinavia by the work of one of the most controversial artists of the period.

Edvard Munch (1863–1944) has often been described as having been a revelation to MacTaggart through the show of his work held in Edinburgh in 1931. But, as a friend of Fanny, it is clear that MacTaggart knew Munch's work before this exhibition. It was MacTaggart and Morton in fact, as members of the SSA's loan works committee, who proposed the show. Munch was already familiar to a number of other Scottish artists at the time. There was opposition to the plan to show Munch's work from members who considered the annual exhibition should consist entirely of work by Scottish artists.[28] But, happily, the MacTaggart / Morton camp prevailed and on 8 October 1931 the SSA recorded a 'unanimous recommendation by the Loan Works Committee that 15 pictures by Herr Edvard Munch, Oslo, should be borrowed on condition that one wall was reserved to show this collection together'.[29] In the event, twelve paintings were chosen by Munch and hung by Fanny.[30] Among the most striking were *Melancholy* of 1900 [figure 13], *The Waves* and *Bohemian Wedding*.[31]

Interest in the loan exhibition was widespread and the SSA's funds were boosted considerably by the attendance figures. According to the catalogue 'no examples of Munch's work' had been shown before in Scotland. He had, it was stated, 'long been the subject of controversy in Continental Art Circles'.[32] Now it was Scotland's turn. The controversy was predictably heated. 'If this is called Modern Art', ranted one correspondent, 'then God help us!'.[33]

Some SSA members actually resigned. Munch's work, so characteristically Scandinavian, provoked a famous debate on the 'Scottishness' of Scottish art which involved some of the principal figures of the 'Scots renaissance', spearheaded by Hugh MacDiarmid. Herbert Read, then Professor of Fine Art at Edinburgh University, declared on radio that Munch's 'nordic sensibility' should be that shared by Scottish artists who had tended in the past to look to France.[34] It was, he declared, the natural inclination of a northern people. That

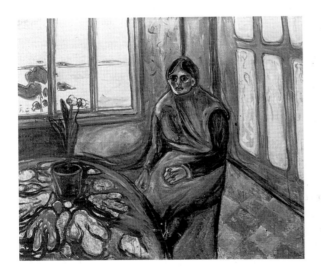

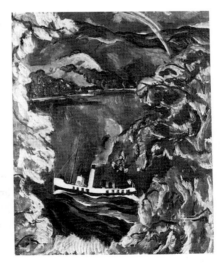

figure 13 *left*
Edvard Munch
Melancholy, 1900
oil on canvas,
110 × 126cm
Munch Museum, Oslo

figure 14 *right*
William MacTaggart
After the Storm, Loch Tay,
circa 1931, oil on canvas,
127 × 101.6cm
Perth Museum and Art
Gallery

MacTaggart embraced this view is shown by the fact that in 1934, as President of the SSA, he brought an exhibition of work by Paul Klee to Edinburgh. Read also now became better acquainted with MacTaggart's work, visiting the private exhibition he held at Hillwood, the family home, in 1932.

The repercussions of the Munch exhibition were widespread. In the art of Gillies it resulted in the introduction of a more violent palette – livid skies and a new emotional response to the landscape, in the Romantic tradition. For MacTaggart, intense exposure to Munch at first hand brought about the acceleration of a change which had been taking place for some time. From the start, *The Ploughed Field* had demonstrated if not a direct debt, then certainly an empathy with the spirit of Van Gogh. It was as if over the past twelve years MacTaggart had repressed this urge and it was Munch who had freed it.[35] Now his composition became increasingly simple, his motif more highly defined and painted, not in a planar style, but echoing in its form the decorative, Secessionist sinuousness of the Norwegian's landscapes. While it would be foolish to attribute to MacTaggart the depth of symbolic content present in Munch, it cannot be entirely denied. What he achieved was more a fusion between the observed landscape and its emotional effect upon the spirit.

It is instructive to compare MacTaggart's 1931–2 painting, *After the Storm, Loch Tay* [figure 14], with his previous work. The central subjects of the puffer, the rainbow and the way in which the foliage acts as a frame are all deeply reminiscent of Munch. The lasting influence, though, is more evident perhaps in *At Longniddry*, MacTaggart's diploma work for the RSA painted about 1938 [plate 8]. A view of a house with a screen of trees, it is strikingly claustrophobic and this single group of isolated buildings becomes a recurrent theme in MacTaggart's work. *The Old Mill, East Linton* [plate 10], painted about 1942 – ten years on from MacTaggart's first close acquaintance with

Munch – is particularly clear evidence of his impact. So close indeed are some of MacTaggart's works to the spirit of Munch that all they appear to lack are figures. Often it seems as if the absence of the figure of a woman tearing her hair or a man with his head buried in despair is all that sets MacTaggart's work apart from the Norwegian's melancholia. Of course, MacTaggart was known for the absence of figures in his work and, when they are included, such as the nuns crossing Edinburgh's Drummond Place [plate 9], it is as a compositional element.

It is significant that, whereas in Munch's work a house is often painted with attention to the windows – what have been termed its 'eyes'[36] – MacTaggart omits such details, absorbing the general feeling of transferred emotion, without identifying with it any more deliberately. Of course, from the 1950s, MacTaggart was to use windows in a way which was purely his own, making them frames for his still lifes, set against a landscape or town street and thus, in a sense, reversing the central idea of Munch. This might stand as a paradigm for the difference between the two artists – the one essentially introspective, the other, MacTaggart, more concerned with searching his soul by looking outside his own human parameters.

Perhaps the greatest effect of the exposure to Munch on MacTaggart's work was the adoption of vibrant, intense colour which presages the great work of the 1950s and his maturity. It was no coincidence that two years after the Munch exhibition and the associated debate about a national school of art that MacTaggart was elected President of the SSA.

Apart from Munch, another artist appears to have had an influence on MacTaggart's development during the 1930s and 1940s. Quite when MacTaggart first saw the work of Matthew Smith (1879–1959) is unclear. It seems likely, though, that he might have known it before 1932. According to MacTaggart's biographer, Henry Harvey Wood,[37] he was aware of it before 1924 when he chanced to meet, in Cassis, the artist's wife,

Gwen. Wood may be wrong here; he describes her as charming and of early middle age (she was forty-eight) and says that she was returning to London for her husband's first solo show – which was in fact in April 1926.[38] It is interesting, though, that Gwen too had studied under Lhote in Paris in 1928–9 and that Smith was also there by early October 1929. We also know that Smith was in Scotland in August 1933 and that he painted a landscape near Biggar, twenty-six miles south of Edinburgh. It is possible, when their work is compared [figures 15 and 16], that it was Smith, as much as Munch, who acted as a catalyst for MacTaggart's distinctive flower pieces of the 1930s.

It is uncertain quite when, during the 1930s, Fanny broke off her engagement to Morton. What is known is that in 1937 William and Fanny were married at his brother's house in Morningside on the prosperous south side of Edinburgh. The honeymoon was spent in Paris, Berlin and Scandinavia – a blissful prelude to the close, happy marriage which lasted until MacTaggart's death forty-four years later. If the burst of colour which invades MacTaggart's painting from this time is formally due to Munch and Smith, it can also be taken as a metaphor for the new colour brought to his life by Fanny. Soon after their marriage the couple bought the Georgian town house at 4 Drummond Place, where they were to live for the next forty years. With this move at the age of thirty-five MacTaggart can be said to have entered on his mature career.

The MacTaggarts lived an ordered life. Both delighted in the variety and the exuberance of art and were constantly attending private views and exhibitions. MacTaggart's studio, on his death, was found to be piled with exhibition catalogues from London, Paris and New York. Significantly, among the other works were tomes on Lhote, Munch, Derain and Cubism. Every year, save those during the war, William and

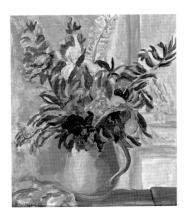

figure 15 William MacTaggart
From my Garden, circa 1935
catalogue 11

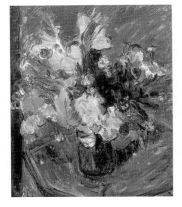

figure 16 Matthew Smith
Flowers with a Light Blue Background,
1928, oil on canvas, 61 × 50.8cm,
private collection

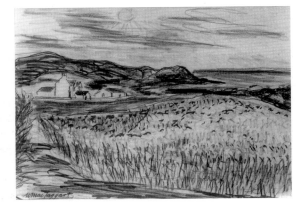

figure 17 William MacTaggart
Port Logan, circa 1968
catalogue 43

Fanny would travel to Scandinavia for the summer, and from 1951 spend every Christmas they could at Johnstounburn Hotel at Humbie, to the south of Edinburgh. Wherever they travelled, frequently in the company of other artist friends including Gillies, William would paint. Often he would merely make charcoal sketches [figure 17] and the merit of these, like his lithographs and watercolours, has never been fully discussed.[39] For an artist who has too often been described as a poor draughtsman, they are spontaneous and lively with a natural command of line as engaging as the colour of his finished oils. Indeed, it might be argued that, together with the very small oil paintings on board which he was fond of executing [plate 17], they are among the most spontaneous manifestations of an art which was based largely upon intuition.

During the war years MacTaggart worked strenuously to encourage the arts, organising in 1941 an exhibition of *Scottish Scenes by Scottish Artists* which might be described as a homegrown version of the 'Recording Britain' project.[40] And, as William painted, Fanny devoted herself to the war effort, travelling, much to his consternation, to the BBC in blitz-torn London, to broadcast to her occupied homeland and help with various Norwegian servicemen's charities. She also seems to have been involved in the courageous 'Shetland Run'.[41] Certainly, after the war, she was decorated by the King of Norway.

Immediately the war came to an end, Fanny and William travelled to Norway[42] and gradually resumed their earlier practice of making prolonged annual visits to rural France. Every summer from 1947 to 1953, they made their base at a small hotel in Orry-la-Ville, half an hour from Paris. It was in the course of one of these trips in 1952 that they visited the major retrospective of the work of Georges Rouault (1871–1958) at the Musée d'Art Moderne in Paris.

Rouault had been described by Roger Fry as early as 1919 as 'a visionary' whose expression was based on 'a profound knowledge of appearances'.[43] As recently as 1935 Rouault had been considered too avant garde for inclusion in Britain's national collections.[44] A late pupil of Gustave Moreau (1826–98), Rouault had never entirely outgrown the influence of the arch-Symbolist. Indeed, his intensely religious, evangelising zeal lies behind his prostitute series of 1903–7. It was Rouault's aim to use colour to express emotion. His style is characterised by the use of heavy black lines [figure 18] that recall the lead of stained glass in church windows. Similarly, there is surely something of religious iconography in both the form and the strident reds, blues and yellows of the still-life paintings that MacTaggart produced from the 1950s. In these, the central motif of a vase of flowers is presented framed by a window (generally that of his own house in Drummond Place) against the night sky. Although MacTaggart was later to say that it was not the religious element of Rouault's work which intrigued him, but 'simply his way of using paint … how he got one colour against another',[45] he did paint at least one tell-tale work in the late 1950s or 1960s whose central motif is the figure of the Virgin.[46] For MacTaggart the most obvious technical influence was Rouault's habit of scrubbing out areas of thick paint, a trait often taken up in his subsequent still lifes. Even under the influence of Rouault, however, MacTaggart continued with his chosen motifs of still life and landscape. Figures were unneccesary. While, as has already been said, it would be foolhardy to attribute MacTaggart's driving force to a conscious Romanticism, it would also be foolish to ignore an undercurrent of theosophical thinking that might – even subconsciously – have underpinned the obsessive concentration on these two subjects in a career spanning some sixty years. It was certainly, to some extent, with the emotional power of colour, as much as the *matière* itself, that MacTaggart was concerned.

This last and longest phase of MacTaggart's career was the most fruitful and the most consistent. It saw him established as one of the grand old men of Scottish art and installed in 1955 as Secretary, and in 1959 as President, of the Royal Scottish Academy. From 1953 to 1962 he served on the Scottish Committee of the Arts Council. From 1960 his work was shown at the Stone Gallery, Newcastle, to great acclaim, alongside such accepted modern masters as Picasso and Moore. In 1961 he received an honorary doctorate from the University of Edinburgh and in 1962 he was awarded a knighthood. MacTaggart was instrumental – with Fanny – in bringing new visual experiences to the people of Scotland. In particular, in 1958, they arranged for an exhibition of Norwegian art to be shown at the Edinburgh Festival. As well as bringing new art to Scotland he and Fanny acted as unofficial cultural ambassadors abroad. In 1955 MacTaggart enjoyed a successful solo show in Oslo. A visit to Germany in 1963 convinced him that were Scotland's arts only allowed the funding given to the rebuilding of Germany's war-torn cultural centres, the nation's art would flourish as never before. MacTaggart's belief in the idea of a specifically Scottish art was a *leitmotif* of his later years, reiterated time and again in newspaper interviews.

Through all these perhaps unforeseen philanthropic incarnations, in which William continually pushed forward the bounds of art and championed his fellow countrymen, Fanny supported his efforts by playing the society hostess. The doors of the drawing room [figure 19] in their elegant New Town house, with its alterations by the architect Robert Lorimer, opened into the dining room to provide a sixty foot reception area. During the 1940s and 1950s, before William had risen to the height of his fame, all was done on a shoe string, although Fanny was skilled at creating a banquet from the most meagre ingredients, often serving her national food and drink – herring and aquavit – to rapturous approval. As Edinburgh grew in international status as a centre for the arts, so Fanny's parties became what can only be described as 'salons'. It was a cosmopolitan society of sparkling wit and talent. Fanny had found herself a position as Scottish arts correspondent for the Nor-

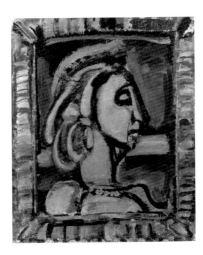

figure 18 *left*
Georges Rouault
Head, circa 1935–40
oil on paper, laid on
canvas, 61.9 × 48.4cm
Scottish National
Gallery of Modern Art

figure 19 *right*
The Drawing Room,
4 Drummond Place,
circa 1962

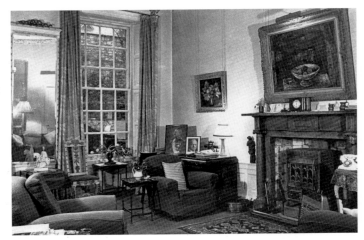

wegian newspaper *Aftenposten* [47] and throughout the 1950s and 1960s she reviewed everything from art exhibitions to ballet and theatre. In the course of her writing, she naturally came to know many of the performers and thus it was that here, surrounded by William's paintings, such celebrities of the period as the MacTaggarts' close friends Benjamin Britten and Peter Pears came into direct contact with neighbours, including Sir Compton Mackenzie,[48] and Edinburgh artists of the time such as Anne Redpath, Robin Philipson (1916–92), William Gillies and John Maxwell (1905–62).

Meanwhile, upstairs in William's studio stood the easel of the elder McTaggart, now used by his grandson. The old man's presence had always been there, although William had never evinced any obvious influence. Having shown a painting – *Blue Sea Machrihanish* – in his first solo show in 1929, it was not until the 1950s that 'MacTaggart Yr' found the confidence to turn his attention to the coastline which had so captivated his grandfather. In such works as *The Gauldrons, Machrihanish* [plate 12], he recalled, perhaps deliberately, the troubled skies of the older painter.

Apart from his achievement as an artist, MacTaggart was also important as an outspoken and forward-thinking educator. He had been given his first teaching post at Edinburgh College of Art in 1933 by Hubert Wellington, the college's liberal principal, who had been taken out to Hillwood by an enthusiastic Herbert Read. The quality which impressed MacTaggart's students most consistently was his gentleness. He was, to quote a critic who knew him well, 'a father figure'.[49] His pleasant disposition seemed to some to contradict work that appeared to embrace such depths of passion. In fact, MacTaggart was subject to black moods and went through a period of appalling nightmares.[50] Continually he emphasised to his pupils the harsh reality of the artist's task. 'Painting', he said in 1961, at the age of fifty-eight, 'gets no easier the longer

you live'.[51] It seemed at times almost as if he were engaged in a physical battle with his art. In 1963 he told an interviewer, 'I am sure that it is often the very fact of struggle which puts the ultimate quality into a work of art'.[52] 'Art', he later said, 'should never be static – what has sometimes been considered the misprint of today becomes the accepted language of tomorrow'.[53]

Throughout this period of intense social and artistic activity, however, MacTaggart was continually plagued by the ill health which had dogged him since childhood. In 1969 he had resigned as President of the RSA, to 'devote more time to his art' and the couples' letters from the 1970s are peppered with references to hospital internments to recover from unspecified, recurrent illnesses.[54] MacTaggart became more seriously ill in the late 1970s and eventually in 1978 he had to cease exhibiting at the RSA. From June of that year he found himself increasingly unable to work. He was, said Fanny, in some distress and 'in need of constant care and attention'.[55] He had already been in one Edinburgh nursing home and by October 1979 was very weak and staying in the Skye Nursing Home at Polwarth Terrace. A return to Drummond Place was unthinkable. The following year he suffered chest troubles and took course after course of antibiotics. Sir William MacTaggart died in hospital in Edinburgh on Friday 9 January 1981 and was cremated five days later at Warriston Crematorium. Nine days later, on 18 January, his beloved Fanny died of a stroke.

It has been suggested that William MacTaggart's career falls into four phases: the first under the influence of Crozier and Lhote, the second under Segonzac, before 1931, the third under Munch – from 1932 to 1952 – and the final under Rouault.[56] The truth is nowhere near as simple. He himself said of the change in his work over half a century, '... there is a progress going on all the time'[57] – and there was. MacTaggart was assimilating ideas continuously. The change, he was later to suggest, was from an analytical, composed idea of painting to a painting of 'a sensation of the flux of experience'.[58] He had wanted, he said, to 'create some kind of mood that somebody responds to.' 'A bouquet of flowers', he said disarmingly, 'I would like to think of simply as a symbol of something ...'.[59]

It would be misguided to over-intellectualise his work. MacTaggart was, above all else, in love with paint. His unique achievement was to maintain an establishment position while at the same time embracing in his painting an avant-garde expressiveness derived from artists on the margins of society. The importance of this to Scottish art has been incalculable. The immediate result was a broadening of minds which might more naturally have been inclined to look to 'safer' forms of art. Happily, such mediocrity was not for William MacTaggart. For him, speaking in his sixty-fifth year, the function of the painter was, as it had always been – 'to enrich the experience of the spectator'.[60]

NOTES AND REFERENCES

1 *The Scotsman*, 10 October 1929.

2 William MacTaggart, in conversation with Douglas Hall, 18 April 1968, Scottish National Gallery of Modern Art Archive.

3 The spelling of the family name had been changed by Hugh, who disliked abbreviations. Cited in a profile of William MacTaggart by Emilio Coia in *Scottish Field*, November 1965.

4 William MacTaggart, in conversation with Douglas Hall, 18 April 1968, Scottish National Gallery of Modern Art Archive.

5 Hugh MacTaggart's business, MacTaggart and Scott, had been founded on the proceeds of a portfolio of work given to him by his father for just that purpose. Information from a conversation between the author and Harriet Macandrew, 20 October 1997.

6 He also had scoliosis (lateral curvature of the spine), known in the family as 'the MacTaggart stoop'.

7 MacTaggart's earliest recorded work is *Moonrise*, bearing the inscription 'painted by Willie when he was 15', present whereabouts unknown. A postcard of Van Gogh's *Cornfield at Pontarmé* is among the papers in the MacTaggart Archive in the National Library of Scotland (NLS, box 17).

8 Quoted in *The Scotsman*, 4 November 1961.

9 Reid had shared a room in Paris with Vincent van Gogh, having been introduced to him by his brother Theo. He also had his portrait painted by Van Gogh. See Duncan Macmillan, *Scottish Art 1460–1990*, Edinburgh, 1990, p.256.

10 William MacTaggart, in conversation with Douglas Hall, 18 April 1968, Scottish National Gallery of Modern Art Archive.

11 Ibid.

12 Ann Simpson, *William Crozier*, Edinburgh, 1995, p.8.

13 *The Scotsman*, 12 October 1923.

14 William MacTaggart, in conversation with Douglas Hall, 18 April 1968, Scottish National Gallery of Modern Art Archive.

15 Philip Long, *William Gillies*, Edinburgh, 1994, p.13.

16 William MacTaggart's obituary, *The Times*, 13 January 1981.

17 A photograph in the MacTaggart Archive (NLS, box 21) shows William and his mother in a gondola on the Grand Canal, Venice, in 1923.

18 They stayed at the Hotel Beaulieu.

19 MacTaggart and Crozier may have painted in the company of Redpath.

20 Ann Simpson, *William Crozier*, Edinburgh, 1995, p.19.

21 *The Scotsman*, December 1927.

22 A photograph in the MacTaggart Archive (NLS, box 20), of a landscape painting by MacTaggart, entitled *Towards Rannoch*, shows a mountainous view, painted very much in Cézanne's style of the 1890s.

23 Soutine's landscapes of the mid 1920s certainly appealed to MacTaggart who kept a number of reproductions of them. MacTaggart Archive (NLS, box 21).

24 This may also echo Crozier's interest in Adam Bruce Thomson, the landscape painter, some fourteen years his senior, who taught him in an evening class at Edinburgh College of Art, instructing him in etching in particular.

25 Henry Harvey Wood, catalogue introduction to William MacTaggart's first solo exhibition at Aitken Dott, Edinburgh, 1929.

26 General Ivar Aavatsmark had been Minister of Defence in the Norwegian government from 1921 to 1923.

27 It has been suggested (William Hardie, *Painting in Scotland 1837 To The Present*, London, 1990, p.161, and Keith Hartley, 'The SSA and its International Connections' in *The*

Society of Scottish Artists, The First 100 Years, ed. Anne Wishart, Edinburgh, 1991, p.32) that it was Morton who proposed the Munch loan exhibition to MacTaggart. But, given MacTaggart's own friendship with Fanny, it might have been a joint initiative. Several photographs in the MacTaggart Archive (NLS, box 21) of paintings by Edvard Munch, bear the inscription on the reverse 'HR Morton' and the dates 'Oslo, summer 1929' and 'Oslo, summer 1931'. Among the works photographed are *The Day After*, 1894; *Ashes*, 1894; *The Frenchman*, 1901. The archive of the Munch Museet, Oslo, contains several letters from Morton to Munch (see Keith Hartley, *Scottish Art since 1900*, Edinburgh and London, 1989, p.46, note 22). The date of Fanny and William's first meeting is mentioned in a report in the *Newcastle Journal* of 6 June 1964 as being at the RSA in Edinburgh in 1931. Family accounts however, contradict this information (conversation between the author and Miss Ann Macandrew, 21 November 1997).

28   The chief voice of opposition was William Macdonald (1883–1960). Noted in the minutes of the Society of Scottish Artists, 21 April 1931 and 27 April 1931.

29   SSA minutes, 8 October 1931.

30   Fanny owned personal photographs of Munch in his studio and outside his house. MacTaggart Archive (NLS, box 21).

31   The twelve exhibited paintings, chosen by Munch himself, were comparatively recent, expressionist works. They were: *Woman in Red*; *The Waves*; *Winter Landscape*; *Landscape*; *The Bathers*; *Bohemian Wedding*; *Lady in Grey*; *Melancholy* (the 1900 version); *Landscape*; *The Forest*; *Galloping Horse*; *Nude*.

32   SSA *Exhibition catalogue*, Edinburgh, 1931, p.25.

33   *The Society of Scottish Artists, The First 100 Years*, ed. Anne Wishart, Edinburgh, 1991, p.13.

34   Read, looking around the SSA show held at the Royal Scottish Academy, in which the works by Munch had been hung, picked out the work of Crozier and MacTaggart as relating to his concept of a specifically nordic art. Keith Hartley, *Scottish Art since 1900*, Edinburgh and London, 1989, p.46.

35   This happened late in 1932. *Paramousquier*, a landscape painted in the autumn of 1931, photograph in the MacTaggart Archive (NLS, box 21) is still closer to the style of Segonzac than that of Munch.

36   Mara Helen Wood in *Edvard Munch, The Frieze of Life*, London, 1992, p.102.

37   Henry Harvey Wood, *W. MacTaggart*, Edinburgh, 1974, p.24.

38   She apparently confided to MacTaggart that 'If this exhibition isn't a success, I don't know what we'll do'. Henry Harvey Wood, *W. MacTaggart*, Edinburgh, 1974, pp.24–5.

39   In the 1950s MacTaggart made single-colour lithographs, often in red on a cream paper, and printed at Harley Brothers, St James's Square, Edinburgh, as Christmas cards from himself and Fanny.

40   The Recording Britain programme was established in 1939, in the face of potential devastation by war. Under Kenneth Clark, it commissioned almost 100 artists of the day to produce, in some 1,500 works, a visual record of Britain. MacTaggart's exhibition *Scottish Scenes by Scottish Artists* was shown 'in the recreation room of a Scottish munitions factory … The same exhibition will tour a number of factories during the next six months', *The Scotsman*, 6 September 1941.

41   The Shetland Run or 'Shetland Bus' was an operation based at Scalloway, on Shetland, during the Second World War, intended for the landing of commando saboteurs on the mainland of German-occupied Norway and, in the other direction, for rescuing endangered members of the Norwegian resistance movement. (Information from *The New Shell Guide to Northern Scotland and the Islands*, Francis Thompson, London, 1987.)

42   Where they were in October 1945. An Oslo exhibition catalogue for that date is in the MacTaggart Archive (NLS, box 20).

43   Roger Fry, *Vision and Design*, 4th edn, London, 1925, p.243.

44   Rouault's painting *Têtes à Massacre* was refused by British galleries as a donation from the Contemporary Art Society as late as 1935.

45   William MacTaggart, in conversation with Douglas Hall, 18 April 1968, Scottish National Gallery of Modern Art Archive.

46   The MacTaggart Archive (NLS, box 20) contains a photograph of a MacTaggart painting of the Virgin, possibly a statue, standing before a moonlit village.

47   Fanny had reviewed the Munch loan exhibition at the SSA (which she had helped curate) in 1931 for the Norwegian press and had mentioned MacTaggart's work.

48   Sir Compton and Lady Mackenzie lived directly across from the MacTaggarts' house, at 10 Drummond Place. Several of MacTaggart's Drummond Place still lifes are known as *Over to Monty's*.

49   Edward Gage, *The Scotsman*, 3 June 1968.

50   Conversation between the author and Harriet Macandrew, 20 November 1997.

51   *The Scotsman*, 4 November 1961.

52   *The Scotsman*, 1 July 1963.

53   *The Scotsman*, 4 March 1969.

54   MacTaggart letters in the RSA archives.

55   Fanny MacTaggart to Robin Philipson, 2 July 1980, from MacTaggart letters in the RSA archives.

56   William Hardie, *Painting in Scotland 1837 To The Present*, London, 1990, p.161.

57   William MacTaggart, in conversation with Douglas Hall, 18 April 1968, Scottish National Gallery of Modern Art Archive.

58   Ibid.

59   Ibid.

60   Ibid.

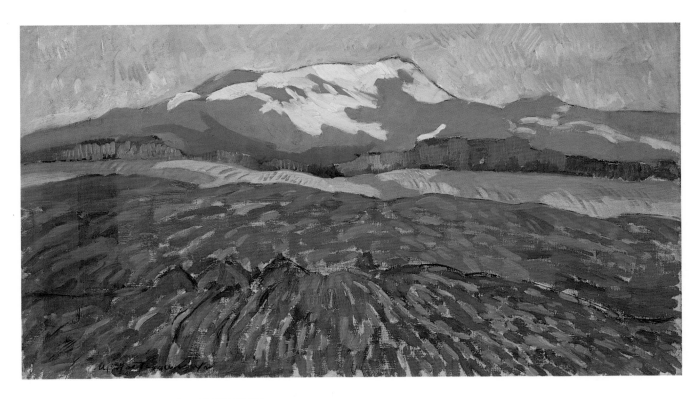

I   THE PLOUGHED FIELD, WOODHOUSELEE

circa 1919 · catalogue 1

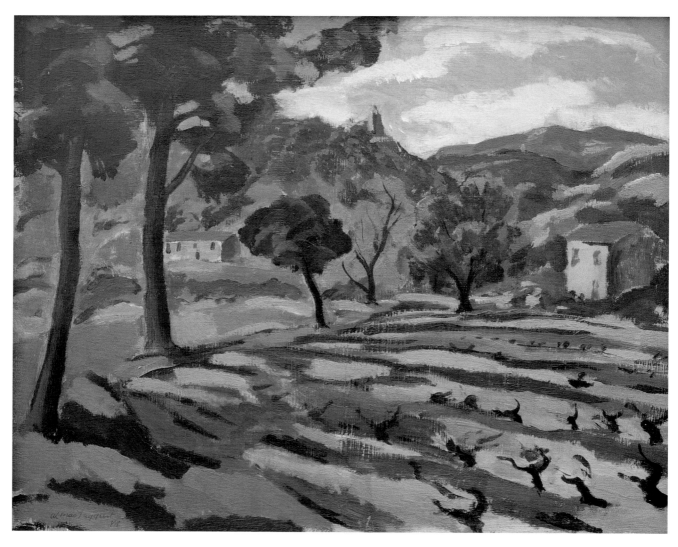

2   GRIMAUD
circa 1924-8 · catalogue 3

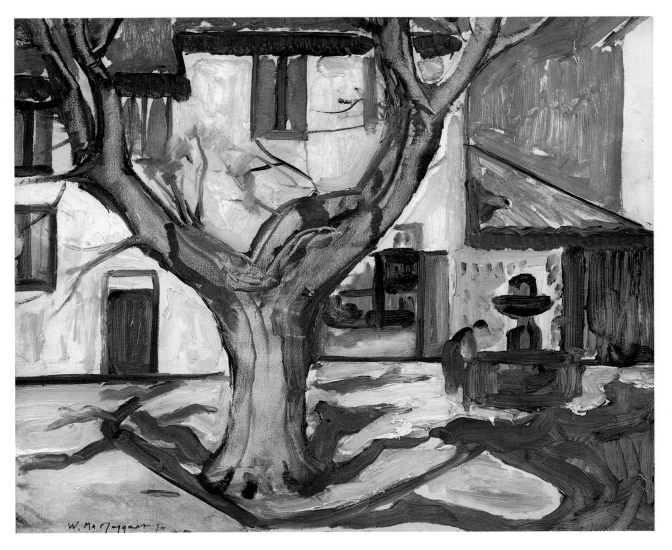

3 FRENCH VILLAGE SQUARE
circa 1924-8 · catalogue 2

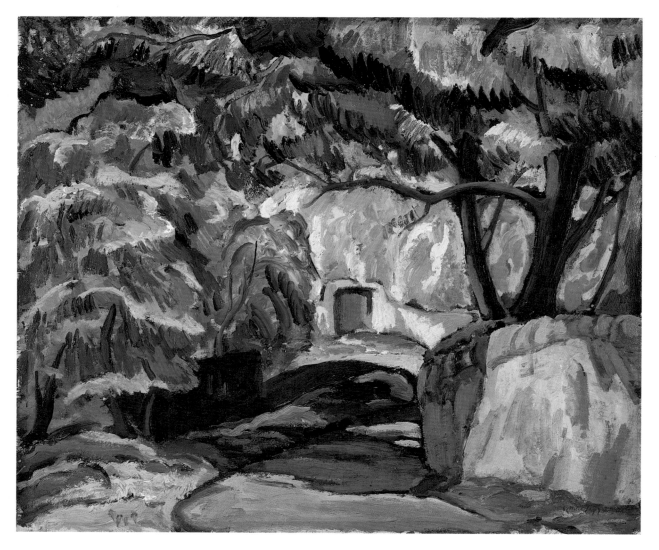

4   THE GATE IN THE WOOD
circa 1926-8 catalogue 5

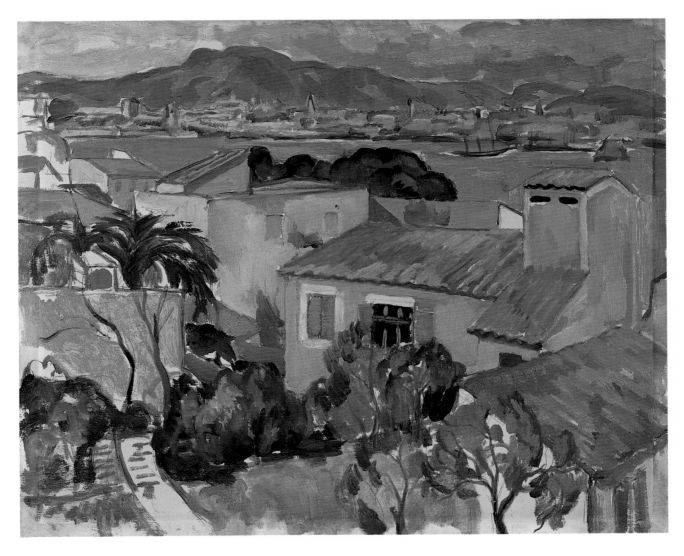

5   CASSIS
circa 1926-8 · catalogue 6

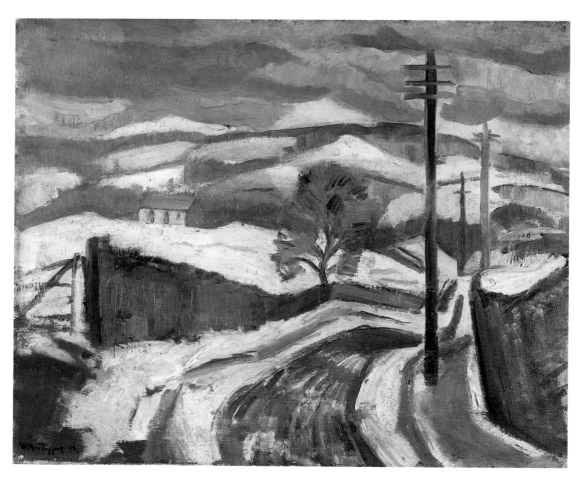

6   SNOW, NEAR LASSWADE
circa 1928 · catalogue 9

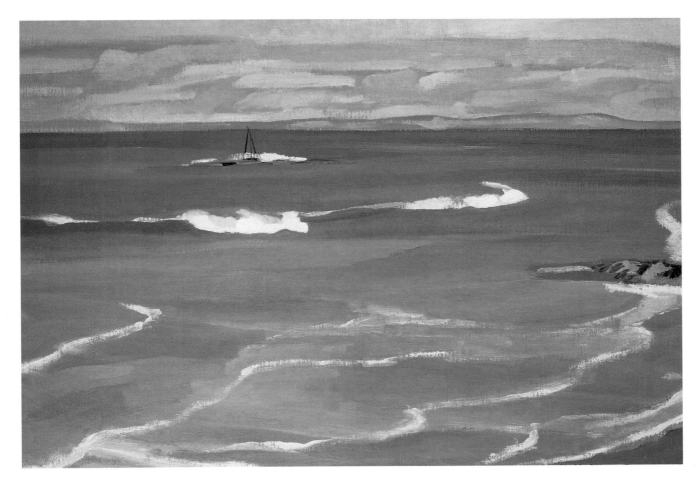

7   THE LOGIE
circa 1929 · catalogue 10

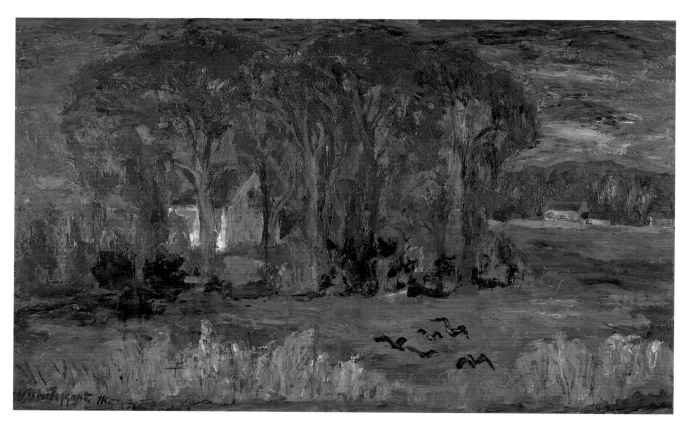

8   AT LONGNIDDRY
circa 1938 · catalogue 13

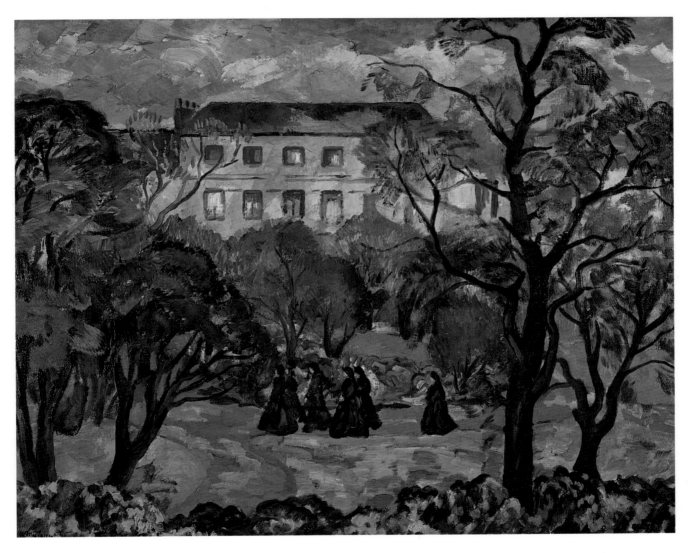

9   THE CONVENT GARDEN
circa 1939 · catalogue 15

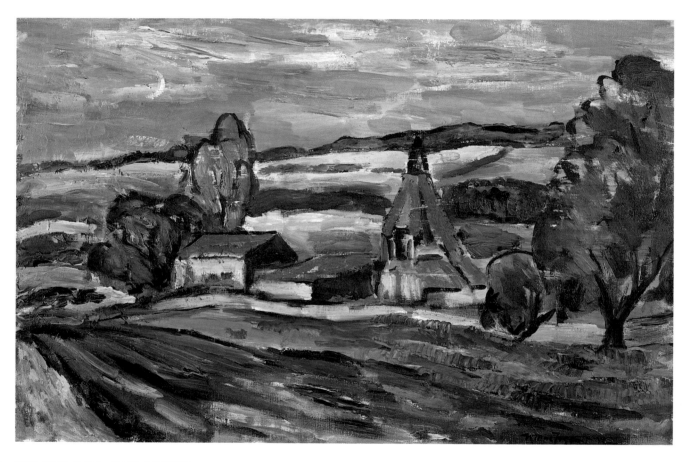

10   THE OLD MILL, EAST LINTON
circa 1942 · catalogue 16

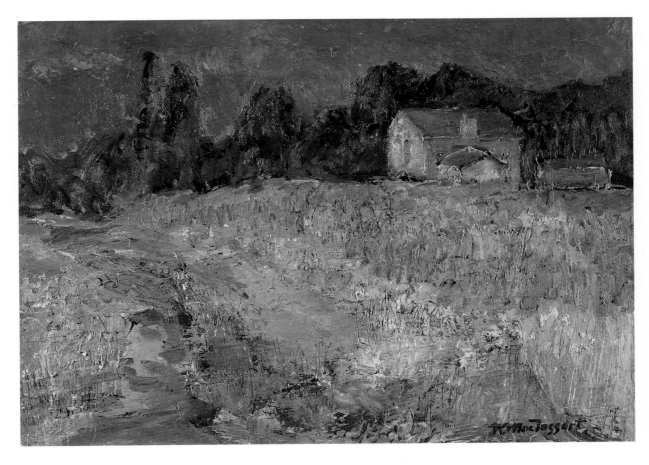

11   FIELDS AT PONTARME
circa 1948 / *circa* 1964 · catalogue 18

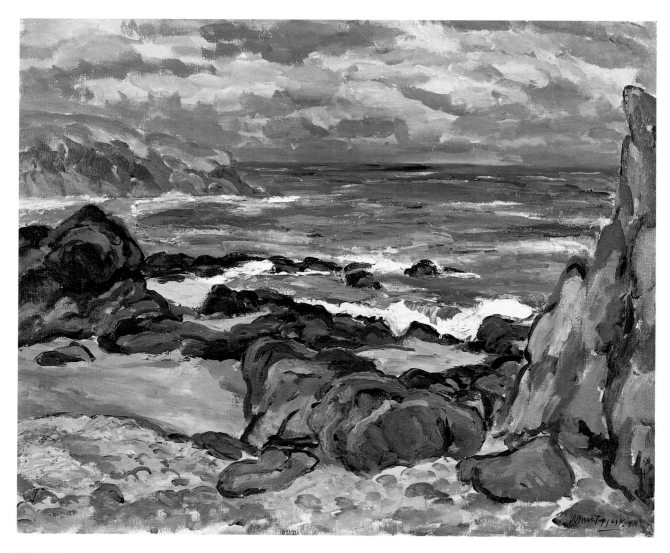

12   THE GAULDRONS, MACHRIHANISH
      1950s · catalogue 20

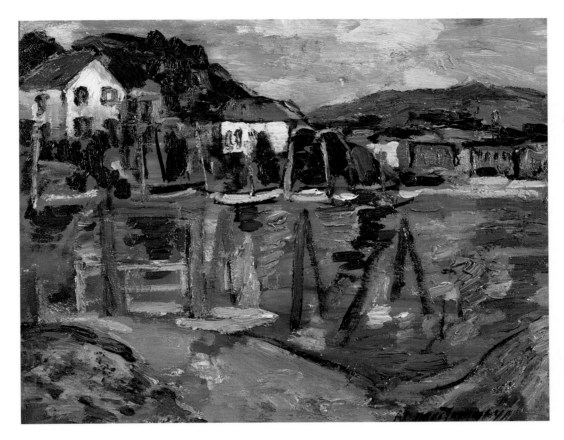

13   ON THE OSLO FJORD
circa 1953 · catalogue 21

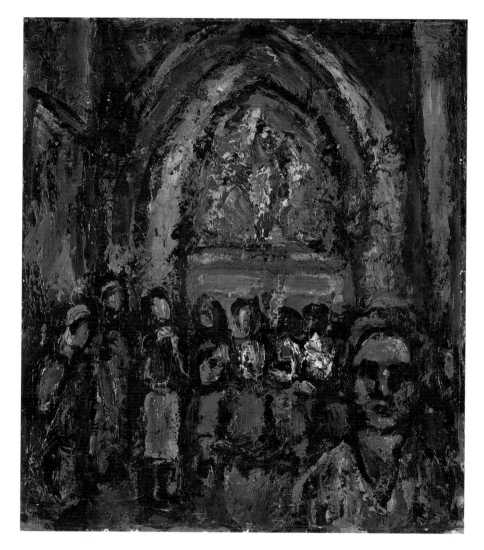

14   YORK MINSTER
1957 · catalogue 23

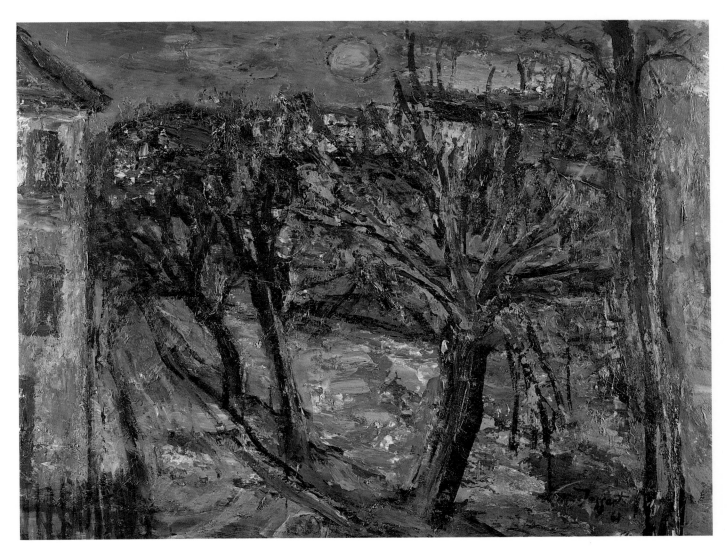

15   ON THE ESK
1961 · catalogue 35

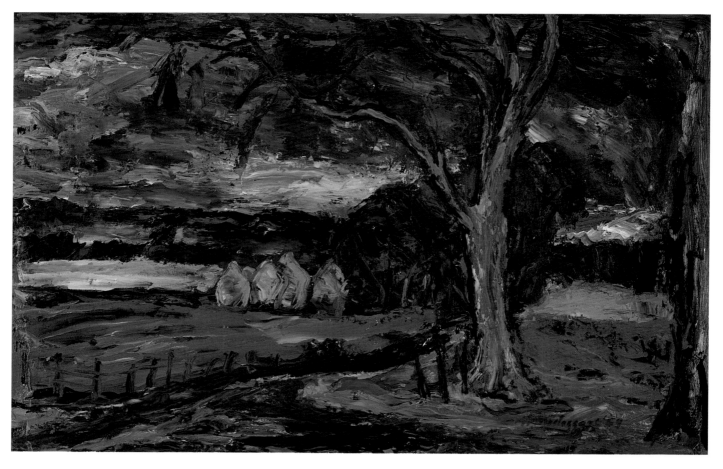

16   NEAR TYNINGHAME
1959 · catalogue 25

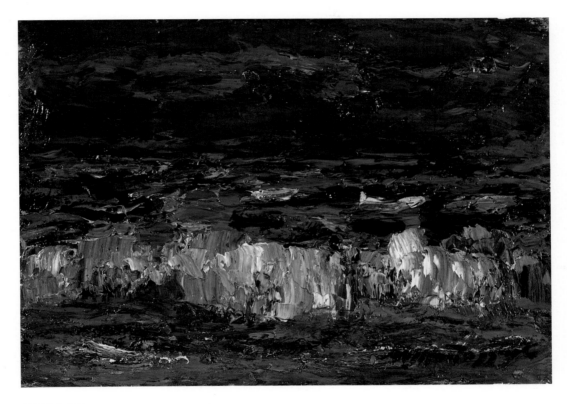

17   ANGRY SEA
circa 1965 · catalogue 41

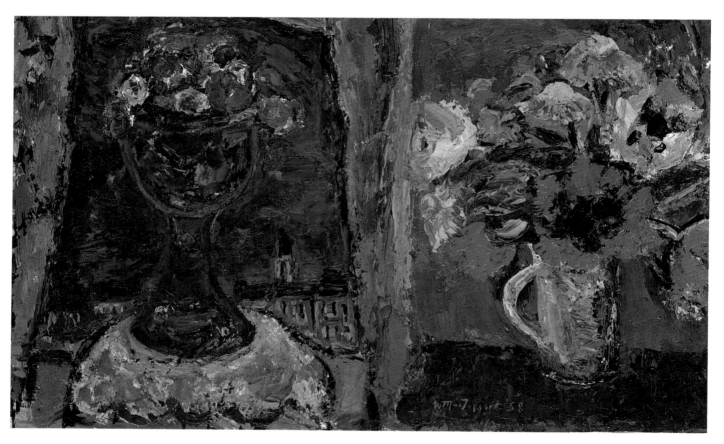

18   DUET
1958 · catalogue 24

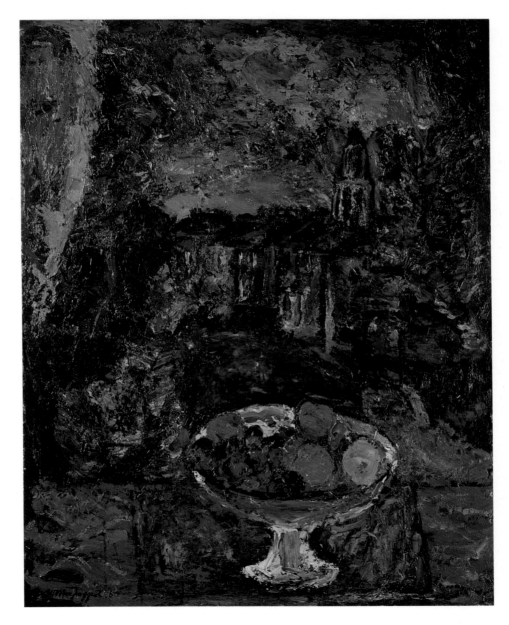

19 THE GLOAMING
1960 · catalogue 29

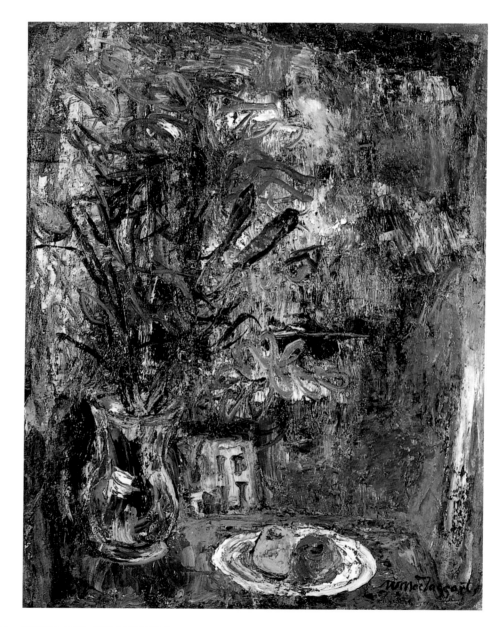

20   TWIGS AND BULLRUSHES

circa 1962 · catalogue 37

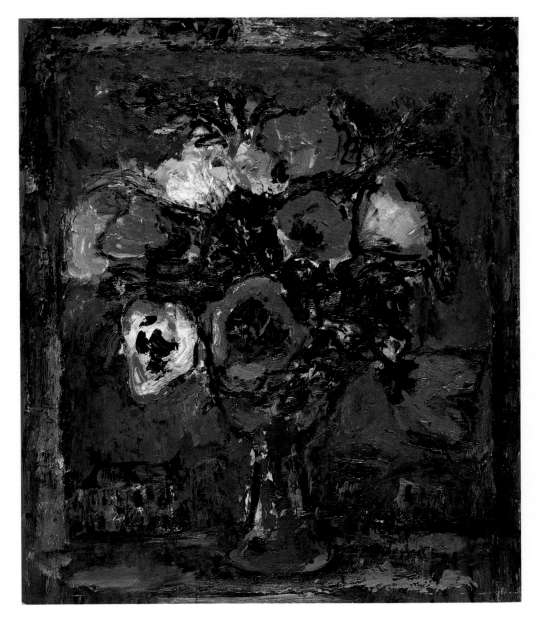

21 POPPIES AGAINST THE NIGHT SKY
circa 1962 · catalogue 36

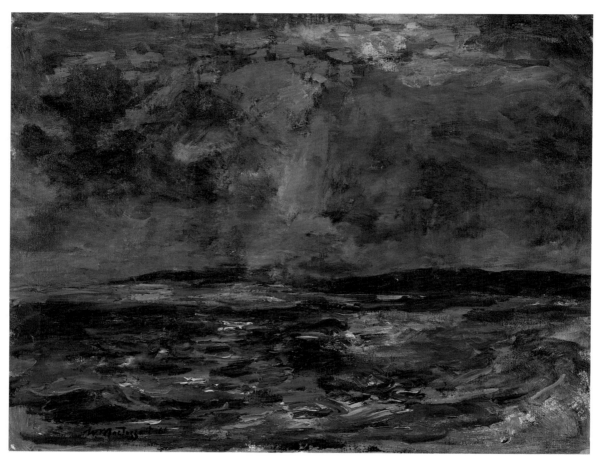

22   STORM CLOUDS
1966 · catalogue 42

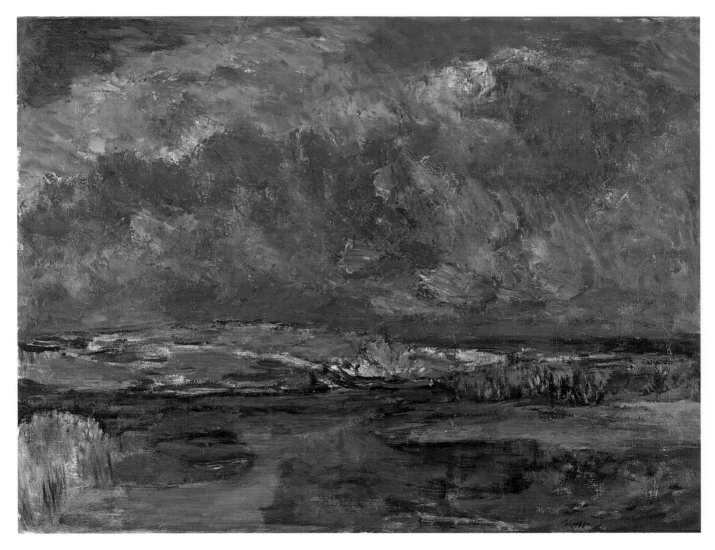

23   THE WIGTOWN COAST
1968 · catalogue 44

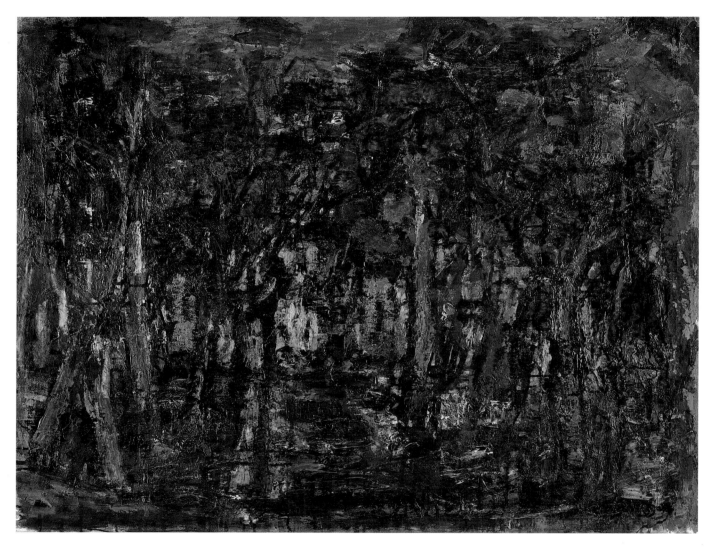

24 NOCTURNE
1963 · catalogue 39

Chronology

1903
William MacTaggart born 15 May at Loanhead near Edinburgh, elder son and third child of Hugh and Roberta MacTaggart (née Little).

1907
Contracted a serious bronchial illness which left him weakened throughout his life. Tutored privately at home.

1910
Death of his grandfather, the painter William McTaggart (b.1835).

1917
Hugh MacTaggart built a studio for his son in the garden of the family home, Hillwood, Loanhead.

1919
Began at Edinburgh College of Art but due to ill health attended only part-time.

1920
Exhibited for the first time at the Royal Glasgow Institute of Fine Arts.

1921
Left Edinburgh College of Art. Exhibited for the first time at the Royal Scottish Academy and the Society of Scottish Artists.

1923
Travelled to France and then to Italy with his mother and visited Florence and Venice. Exhibition of around thirty of his paintings held in the hall of St Andrew's Church, Cannes. Moved to 45 Frederick Street where he shared a studio with William Crozier. Elected Member of the Society of Scottish Artists, then the youngest professional member ever elected. Became a founder member of the exhibiting society the 1922 Group.

1924
In December travelled to Cassis.

1927
Elected to fill vacancy in the Society of Eight, of which Lavery, Cadell and Peploe were members.

1929
First exhibition held at Aitken Dott's, Edinburgh.

1930
Deaths of MacTaggart's father and mother and at the end of the year William Crozier (b.1893). MacTaggart moved out of the Frederick Street studio and returned to the family home in Loanhead.

1931
Twelve works by Edvard Munch exhibited at the annual exhibition of the Society of Scottish Artists.

1932
Exhibition at the family home, Hillwood, Loanhead.

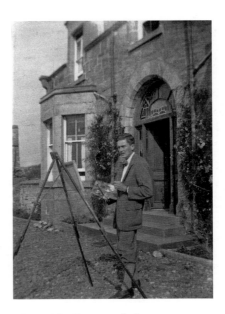

William MacTaggart painting at Gareloch, *circa* 1920

1933
Appointed part-time teacher at Edinburgh College of Art. Elected President of the Society of Scottish Artists.

1934
As President of the Society of Scottish Artists, responsible for an exhibition of work by Paul Klee at the Society's annual exhibition.

1936
Retired as President of the Society of Scottish Artists.

1937
Married Fanny Margaretha Basilier Aavatsmark and spent honeymoon in Paris, Berlin and Scandinavia. Elected Associate of the Royal Scottish Academy.

1938
Moved to 4 Drummond Place in Edinburgh's New Town where he and Fanny lived for the rest of their lives. Exhibition at James Connell & Sons, Glasgow. Work included in the Empire Exhibition, Palace of Art, Bellahouston Park, Glasgow.

1939
Honorary exhibition organiser for Council for the Encouragement of Music and the Arts (until 1945).

1941
Organised an exhibition of work by Scottish artists to tour Scotland's factories.

1945
Travelled to Norway. First exhibition at T. & R. Annan, Glasgow.

1947
Second exhibition at T. & R. Annan.

1948
Elected Academician of the Royal Scottish Academy. Appointed the Royal Scottish Academy's representative on the Council of the Edinburgh International Festival.

1952
Travelled to France and visited repeatedly the Rouault exhibition held in Paris.

1953
Appointed to the Scottish Committee of the Arts Council of Great Britain (until 1962). Second exhibition at Aitken Dott's.

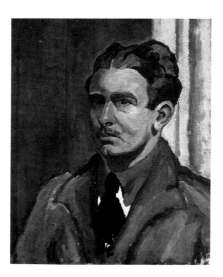

William MacTaggart *Self-portrait, circa* 1935 (catalogue 12)

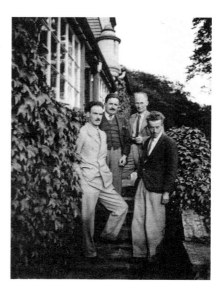

left to right Donald Moodie, William MacTaggart, Adam Bruce Thomson and William Gillies, 1950s

1954
Works included in *Some Edinburgh Painters: R. Henderson Blyth, William Gillies, William MacTaggart, Anne Redpath, William Wilson*, National Gallery of Canada, Ottawa.

1955
Elected Secretary of the Royal Scottish Academy. Exhibition at the Kunstnerforbundet, Oslo. Visited Spain.

1957
Appointed member of the Scottish Advisory Committee of the Independent Television Authority (until 1964).

1958
Organised with Fanny an exhibition of Norwegian art for the Edinburgh International Festival.

1959
Elected President of the Royal Scottish Academy; Honorary Member of the Royal Academy, London; Honorary Royal Hibernian Academician and Honorary Member of the Royal Scottish Society of Painters in Watercolour. Third exhibition at Aitken Dott's.

1960
First exhibition at the Stone Gallery, Newcastle-upon-Tyne. Appointed Trustee of the National Museum of Antiquities, Edinburgh. Represented in exhibition of British art, *70 years of British Painting*, Peking, China.

1961
Received Honorary Doctor of Law from Edinburgh University.

1962
Awarded a knighthood. Second exhibition at the Stone Gallery.

1963
Visited Germany at the invitation of the West German government to observe the country's cultural reconstruction programme. Work included in the exhibition *Four Scottish Painters: Eardley, MacTaggart, Philipson, Redpath* organised by the Scottish Committee of the Arts Council of Great Britain for the Edinburgh International Festival.

1964
Third exhibition at the Stone Gallery. Work included in *Fourteen Scottish Painters*, Commonwealth Institute, London.

1965
Made a Freeman of Loanhead.

1966
Visited Romania as guest of the Romanian Academy of Science and Art. Fourth exhibition at Aitken Dott's.

1967
Elected Fellow of the Royal Society of Edinburgh.

1968
Elected Associate of the Royal Academy, London. Awarded Chevalier de la Légion d'Honneur. Retrospective exhibition at the Scottish National Gallery of Modern Art, later shown in Glasgow and Middlesbrough, organised by the Scottish Arts Council and the National Galleries of Scotland.

1969
Honorary Fellowship of the Royal Incorporation of Architects in Scotland. Resigned as President of the Royal Scottish Academy.

1971
Exhibition at the Loomshop Gallery, Lower Largo, Fife.

1973
Elected Academician of the Royal Academy, London.

1978
Due to ill health, ceased exhibiting at the Royal Scottish Academy.

1981
Died 9 January in hospital. Nine days later his wife, Fanny, died.
Studio sale of MacTaggart's work held by Christie's, Edinburgh.

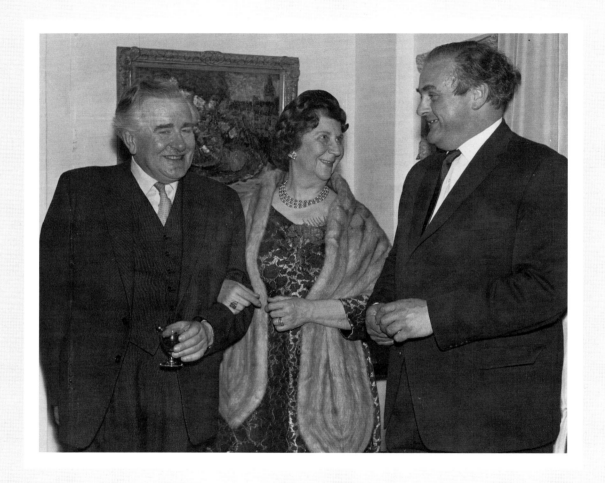

Sir William and Lady MacTaggart with Ronald Marshall of The Stone Gallery, 1962

Bibliography

Emilio Coia, 'Sir William MacTaggart', *Scottish Field*, November 1965

Thomas Elder Dickson, 'William MacTaggart', *The Studio*, October 1959

Edward Gage, *The Scotsman*, 3 June 1968

Sydney Goodsir Smith, 'William MacTaggart', *The Scotsman*, 22 April 1961

Douglas Hall, conversation with Sir William MacTaggart, 18 April 1968, manuscript in Scottish National Gallery of Modern Art Archive

Douglas Hall, *Sir William MacTaggart*, retrospective exhibition catalogue, Edinburgh, 1968

William Hardie, *Painting in Scotland 1837 To the Present*, London, 1990

Keith Hartley, 'The SSA and its International Connections', in *The Society of Scottish Artists, The First 100 Years*, ed. Anne Wishart, Edinburgh, 1991

Keith Hartley, *Scottish Art since 1900*, London and Edinburgh, 1989

W. E. Johnson, *The Guardian*, 28 November 1960

Philip Long, *William Gillies, Watercolours of Scotland*, Edinburgh, 1994

Philip Long, *Anne Redpath*, Edinburgh, 1996

Duncan Macmillan, *Scottish Art 1460–1990*, Edinburgh, 1990

The Newcastle Journal, 6 June 1964

The Scotsman, 12 October 1923

The Scotsman, December 1927

The Scotsman, 10 October 1929

The Scotsman, 6 September 1941

The Scotsman, 4 November 1961

The Scotsman, 1 July 1963

The Scotsman, 4 March 1969

Ann Simpson, *William Crozier*, Edinburgh, 1995

The Times, Obituary of Sir William MacTaggart, 13 January 1981

Henry Harvey Wood, *William MacTaggart*, exhibition catalogue for Aitken Dott's, Edinburgh, 1929

Henry Harvey Wood, *W. MacTaggart*, Edinburgh, 1974

Mara Helen Wood, *Edvard Munch, The Frieze of Life*, London, 1992

The papers from William MacTaggart's estate are held by the National Library of Scotland. Further archival material relating to MacTaggart is in the archives of the Royal Scottish Academy, Scottish National Gallery of Modern Art and the Society of Scottish Artists.

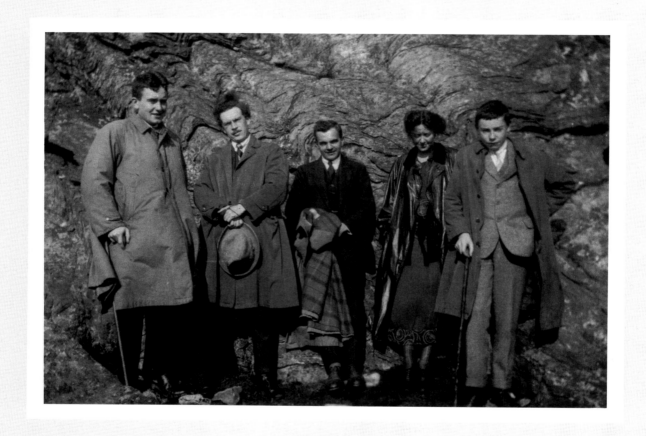

left to right William MacTaggart, William Crozier, Hugh and Margaret MacTaggart and Gordon Macandrew, 1920s

Catalogue

All sizes are given in centimetres, height preceding width.

1
THE PLOUGHED FIELD,
WOODHOUSELEE
circa 1919, plate 1
oil on canvas, 50.4 × 81.3
Mr I.D. Ross

2
FRENCH VILLAGE SQUARE
circa 1924–8, plate 3
oil on panel, 36.5 × 45
Private collection

3
GRIMAUD
circa 1924–8, plate 2
oil on panel, 45.7 × 55.9
Miss Hannah and Miss Hayley Abram

4
LA BOCCA
circa 1925
oil on board, 30.5 × 39
Sir Angus Grossart

5
THE GATE IN THE WOOD
circa 1926–8, plate 4
oil on wood, 60 × 70.3
Mr I.D. Ross

6
CASSIS
circa 1926–8, plate 5
oil on wood, 59.9 × 72.4
Private collection

7
WILLIAM CROZIER
circa 1927
oil on board, 55.5 × 45.1
*Scottish National Portrait Gallery,
presented by the executors of the artist 1981*

8
WADINGBURN
circa 1927
oil on board, 76 × 92
Private collection, London

9
SNOW, NEAR LASSWADE
circa 1928, plate 6
oil on wood, 50.5 × 60.7
*Scottish National Gallery of Modern Art,
purchased 1968*

10
THE LOGIE
circa 1929, plate 7
oil on canvas, 55.9 × 76.2
*Private collection, courtesy Duncan R.
Miller Fine Arts*

11
FROM MY GARDEN
circa 1935, figure 15
oil on board, 59 × 49
*Private collection, courtesy of The Scottish
Gallery, Edinburgh*

12
SELF-PORTRAIT
circa 1935, illustrated p.50
oil on board, 64.2 × 54.2
Private collection

13
AT LONGNIDDRY
circa 1938, plate 8
oil on board, 60.5 × 99.6
Royal Scottish Academy
(Diploma Collection)

14
THE ROAD TO RAYOL
circa 1939
oil on canvas, 43.2 × 53.4
The Scottish Gallery, Edinburgh

15
THE CONVENT GARDEN
circa 1939, plate 9
oil on canvas, 99 × 125
Mr Magnus Linklater and Lady Linklater

16
THE OLD MILL, EAST LINTON
circa 1942, plate 10
oil on canvas, 51 × 76.2
Scottish National Gallery of Modern Art,
bequeathed by Dr R.A. Lillie 1977

17
CORNFIELD, PONTARME
circa 1948–9
oil on board, 62.1 × 101
City of Aberdeen Art Gallery and
Museums Collections

18
FIELDS AT PONTARME
circa 1948 / *circa* 1964, plate 11
oil on board, 51.4 × 71.2
Scottish National Gallery of Modern Art,
Scott Hay Collection, presented 1967

19
SOME YELLOW FLOWERS
circa 1950
oil on canvas, 73 × 53.5
City Art Centre, Edinburgh, Scottish Arts
Council Bequest 1997

20
THE GAULDRONS,
MACHRIHANISH
1950s, plate 12
oil on canvas, 76.5 × 91.5
Private collection

21
ON THE OSLO FJORD
circa 1953, plate 13
oil on board, 32 × 41
Private collection

22
WINTER SUNSET – THE RED SOIL
1956
oil on canvas, 69.9 × 90.2
Arts Council Collection, Hayward Gallery,
London

23
YORK MINSTER
1957, plate 14
oil on board, 60 × 50
Bourne Fine Art, Edinburgh

24
DUET
1958, plate 18
oil on board, 61 × 101
Tate Gallery, presented by the Trustees of
the Chantrey Bequest 1960

25
NEAR TYNINGHAME
1959, plate 16
oil on panel, 61 × 91.5
Robert Fleming Holdings Limited

26
ROSES
1959
oil on board, 53.4 × 40.6
Scottish National Gallery of Modern Art,
bequeathed by Miss Tertia Liebenthal 1970

27
FROSTY SUNSET, HUMBIE
1960
oil on board, 71 × 91.5
The University of Edinburgh

28
DANISH HARBOUR
circa 1960, cover illustration
oil on board, 40 × 51
Private collection

29
THE GLOAMING
1960, plate 19
oil on board, 91 × 71
Duncan R. Miller Fine Arts

30
FLOWERS AND FRUIT
(DRUMMOND PLACE)
1960
oil on canvas, 91.4 × 71.1
Tom Bell Fine Art, Troon

31
SUNSET
circa 1960
oil on board, 12.7 × 17.8
Cyril Gerber Fine Art

32
CANDLES AND FRUIT
circa 1960
oil on board, 55.2 × 76
Private collection

33
HARVEST LANDSCAPE
1960s
oil on board, 63.5 × 76.2
Private collection

34
REFLECTIONS
1960s
oil on canvas, 84.5 × 110
*Argyll and Bute Council, Campbeltown
Museum, Scottish Arts Council Bequest
1997*

35
ON THE ESK
1961, plate 15
oil on board, 71.1 × 91.5
*Scottish National Gallery of Modern Art,
Scott Hay Collection, presented 1967*

36
POPPIES AGAINST THE NIGHT
SKY
circa 1962, plate 21
oil on board, 76.2 × 63.5
*Scottish National Gallery of Modern Art,
Scott Hay Collection, presented 1967*

37
TWIGS AND BULLRUSHES
circa 1962, plate 20
oil on canvas, 91.5 × 71.5
Private collection

38
AWAY TO THE WEST
1963
oil on canvas, 86.4 × 111.8
*Private collection, courtesy Bourne Fine
Art, Edinburgh*

39
NOCTURNE
1963, plate 24
oil on canvas, 86.4 × 111.7
*Scottish National Gallery of Modern Art,
purchased (Gulbenkian UK Trust Fund)
1963*

40
CORNFIELDS
1964
oil on board, 63.5 × 76.2
*Scottish National Gallery of Modern Art,
Scott Hay Collection, presented 1967*

41
ANGRY SEA
circa 1965, plate 17
oil on board, 18 × 25.5
The Blythswood Gallery, Glasgow

42
STORM CLOUDS
1966, plate 22
oil on canvas, 71.2 × 91.5
City Art Centre, Edinburgh

43
PORT LOGAN
circa 1968, figure 17
charcoal and black ink on paper,
27.5 × 39
Private collection

44
THE WIGTOWN COAST
1968, plate 23
oil on canvas, 86.2 × 111.5
Scottish National Gallery of Modern Art,
purchased 1983

45
POPPIES AGAINST THE NIGHT
SKY
circa 1971
oil on board, 60 × 49.5
Private collection

46
SKETCHBOOK
pencil and pastel on paper, 24 × 15.2
Scottish National Gallery of Modern Art,
presented by the executors of the artist 1981

47
SKETCHBOOK
pastel and charcoal on paper, 29.2 × 19
Scottish National Gallery of Modern Art,
presented by the executors of the artist 1981

48
SKETCHBOOK
charcoal, pencil and ink on paper,
26 × 19.6
Scottish National Gallery of Modern Art,
presented by the executors of the artist 1981

49
SKETCHBOOK
charcoal on paper, 35 × 24.7
Scottish National Gallery of Modern Art,
presented by the executors of the artist 1981

50
SKETCHBOOK
charcoal and chalk on paper, 35.5 × 25.1
Scottish National Gallery of Modern Art,
presented by the executors of the artist 1981

51
SKETCHBOOK
charcoal and ink on paper, 35.5 × 25.1
Scottish National Gallery of Modern Art,
presented by the executors of the artist 1981

52
SKETCHBOOK
charcoal, chalk and pencil on paper,
35.5 × 24.7
Scottish National Gallery of Modern Art,
presented by the executors of the artist 1981

53
Benno Schotz 1891–1984
WILLIAM MACTAGGART
circa 1970
bronze, 70.5 × 59 × 34 (including base)
Royal Scottish Academy

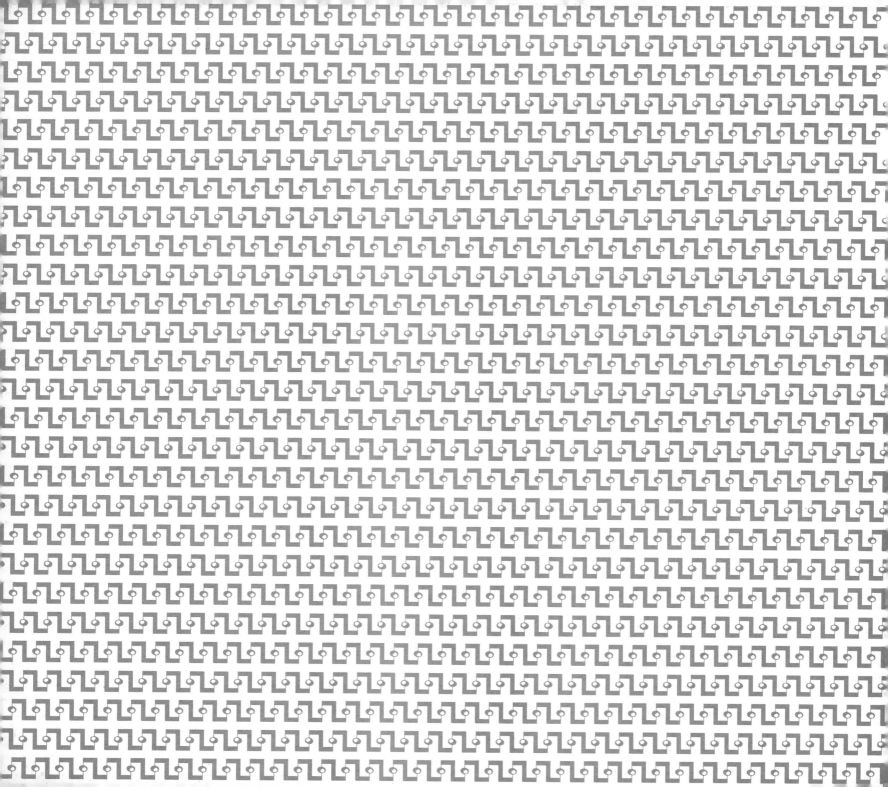